E⌐ ⌐N

E⌐ ⌐N

Published by The Word Among Us Press
7115 Guilford Road
Frederick, Maryland 21704
www.wau.org

ISBN: 978-1-59325-212-0

Scripture texts used in this work are taken from the Revised
Standard Version Bible: Catholic Edition, copyright © 1965
and 1966; and the New Revised Standard Version: Catholic
Edition, copyright © 1989, both by the Division of Christian
Education of the National Council of the Churches of Christ
in the United States of America.
All rights reserved. Used with permission.

Cover design by David Crosson
Cover image: AgnusImages.com
This Holy Renderings monstrance is loosely based on a French
19th centruy Art Nouveau monstrance by Thomas-Joseph
Armand-Calliat of Lyon, France. The original can be seen at
the Basilica of Montmartre in Paris, France.

Made and printed in the United States of America

ABOUT THIS PAMPHLET

The Word Among Us is delighted to present three articles that unfold for us the profound gift of himself that Jesus has given us in the Eucharist and how we can fix our hearts on him in Eucharistic adoration. Taken from the June 2006 issue of our monthly devotional magazine, the articles in this pamphlet will help us to encounter Jesus personally in the Blessed Sacrament and in the time we spend worshipping him in his Eucharistic presence.

The first selection, "Come and See," examines the "divine logic" behind Eucharistic adoration and some of the miracles that strengthen our faith in Jesus' real presence in the Eucharist. In the second, "With Eyes Wide Open," we see how Jesus wants to touch us deeply, speak to us, heal us, and transform us when we meet him in adoration. In the final article, "Love Is Blind," we meditate on how Jesus fixes his gaze of love on us and draws us closer to himself when we come before him in the Blessed Sacrament.

As we reflect on these articles and enter into Jesus' presence, may our love for him be enkindled and may our gratitude for the great gift he has given us in the Eucharist overflow in heartfelt praise and thanksgiving.

COME AND SEE

Human reason and logic are wonderful gifts from God. Without them, we wouldn't be able to survive. And like all the other gifts he has given, God wants to see us develop these as well. He loves watching us apply clear thinking to all aspects of our lives: our families, our work, even our faith. He wants us to learn how to "reason in faith" by taking the truths he has revealed to us and applying them to our own philosophy of life and to the decisions we face every day.

Yet even as God wants us to use our reasoning skills, he also knows that logic alone can be quite limiting. He knows that it defies human logic to believe that simple bread and wine can be transformed into the body and blood of Christ. He knows that it is illogical to hold that the consecrated host remains forever transformed into Christ, even if it is sitting unattended in a tabernacle or is placed in a monstrance for adoration.

It is in situations like these that God asks us to submit our logic, as good as it is, to the revealed truths of faith. And that's just what we want to do in this booklet. We want to ask the Holy Spirit to help us believe more strongly in Jesus' presence in the Blessed Sacrament. We want to ask him to fill us with the blessings, the joy, and the grace that are waiting for us as we spend time with Jesus in Eucharistic adoration.

Miracles Can Help. Around the year 700, there was a priest in Lanciano, Italy, who was struggling with his faith in the presence of Christ in the Eucharist. One morning, while celebrating Mass, he was astonished to see the host change into real flesh and the wine into real blood. His initial shock gave way to joy as he proclaimed to those near him: "Behold the flesh and the blood of our most beloved Christ!"

Diego de Atienzia, (Active mid 17th CE) Monstrance. 1646/9.
Silver gilt with enamel, cast, chased, and engraved. Photo credit: Image
copyright Photo credit: The Metropolitan Museum of Art / Art Resource, NY

After repeated and thorough investigations, scientists have concluded that the flesh and blood actually do belong to the human species. More specifically, the flesh consists of myocardial tissue (the muscular tissue of the heart wall), and the blood contains just the right proteins in the same proportions as normal human blood. Even though this miracle occurred thirteen centuries ago, both the flesh and blood remain intact and are on display in the Church of St. Francis in Lanciano.

More than five hundred years later, in 1263, a German priest, Peter of Prague, decided to take a pilgrimage to Rome—again, to ask God to deepen his faith. On the way, he stopped in the town of Bolsena, Italy, where he celebrated Mass. What began as a normal liturgy, however, took a miraculous turn when Fr. Peter raised the host he had just consecrated. Real blood began to trickle from the host, over his hands, and onto the altar cloth.

After nearly a year of investigation and authentication, the miracle was confirmed, and the blood-stained corporal was brought to the church at Orvieto, where Pope Urban IV was living at the time. The corporal is still on display there and attracts thousands of worshippers each year. It has been said that this miracle is what prompted Urban to institute the feast of the Body and Blood of Jesus, or Corpus Christi, a year after the miracle occurred.

It really is Jesus strengthening us and renewing us in his love, his joy, and his peace.

Sometimes God gives us miracles like these to help strengthen our faith in his promises. When he walked among us, Jesus said that he would give us his flesh to eat and his blood to drink. What's more, he promised that those who ate his flesh and drank his blood would have eternal life. So these miracles, and others like them, exist to spur us on and to help convince us that the Eucharist really is Jesus feeding us and helping us to live holy and pleasing lives. It really is Jesus strengthening us and renewing us in his love, his joy, and his peace. It really is Jesus empowering us to bear fruit for him.

Why Eucharistic Adoration? The basilica at Orvieto and the church in Lanciano are popular places of pilgrimage. At both spots, the miraculous elements are on display, and believers come from all over the world to pray before them. They come because they want to be close to Jesus and taste his unconditional love. They want to be reminded of what he did for us on the cross. They want to be healed and to have their prayers answered. They want to hear what the Holy Spirit might have to say to them.

But we don't have to go to Italy or other places where similar miracles have occurred—at least not if we just want to be in Jesus' presence. He is present in our own churches. And what's even better, he who is present wants to make himself known to us!

These miracles—and the devotions that have sprung up around them—show us that we don't have to limit ourselves to the Mass if we want to experience Jesus in this most intimate way. Pope John Paul II urged that the "worship given to the Trinity . . . must fill our churches outside of the timetable of Masses." He went on to say that "adoration of Christ in this sacrament of love must find expression in the various forms of Eucharistic devotion. . . . Let us be generous with our time in going to meet him in adoration and in contemplation that is full of faith" (*Dominicae Cenae*, 3).

Likewise, St. Alphonsus Liguori conveyed his own experience of Eucharistic adoration when he wrote: "It is sweet to everyone to be in the company of a dear friend. Shall we not find it sweet, in this valley of tears, to remain in the company of the best friend we have, who can do us every kind of good, who loves us with the most tender affection and therefore dwells always with us? Behold, in the Blessed Sacrament we can converse at pleasure with Jesus, we can open our hearts to him, we can lay our wants before him, and we can ask him for his graces. In a word, in this sacrament we can treat with the king of heaven, in all confidence and without restraint" (*Visits to the Blessed Sacrament*, 19).

"Come and See." When Philip invited Nathanael to come meet Jesus with him, he told his friend: "We have found him about whom Moses in the law and also the prophets wrote, Jesus son of Joseph from Nazareth." When Nathanael scoffed and asked, "Can anything good come out of Nazareth?" Philip replied simply, "Come and see." Nathanael did just that, and within the first few moments of his conversation with Jesus, he declared, "Rabbi, you are the Son of God! You are the King of Israel!" (John 1:45-46,49).

Brothers and sisters, what happened to Nathanael can happen to us. When we "come and see" Jesus in the Blessed Sacrament, he will convince us that he is the Son of God, that he is our Savior, and that he is our Lord. The same Jesus who changed Nathanael can change our lives as we spend time in his presence.

But it won't happen as if by magic. Of course, God will bless us if we just show up and sit passively before him, but there is so much more available to us than a general blessing from God. As we said at the beginning of this article, God loves it when we use our intellect and logic. He loves it even more when we use our intellect in prayer, holding fast to the truths of Christ's presence and telling ourselves to expect Jesus to touch us and teach us.

Jesus promised that "all who see the Son *and believe in him* may have eternal life" (John 6:40, emphasis ours). That active belief is what will bring us into contact with Jesus. It will open the floodgates of his blessing and his love for us.

So when you go to visit Jesus in the Blessed Sacrament, ask him to raise up your human logic and fill it with the logic of divine love. Ask him to reveal himself to you, and listen for his still, small voice in your heart. After all, prayer is conversation with God—conversation with a God who loves to talk with us and to embrace us with his love. ■

God will bless us if we just show up and sit passively before him, but there is so much more available to us than a general blessing from God.

WITH EYES WIDE OPEN

....

ENCOUNTERING THE LORD IN ADORATION

Which of the following people actually encountered Jesus when they came to their church and sat before the Blessed Sacrament in adoration?

The young boy who stopped in on his way home from school just to say "hello" to Jesus. The man who slipped into the back of the church and repented over and over again for the way he had sinned against the Lord. The teenager who said the Our Father, the Hail Mary, and the Glory Be three times. The woman who said four rosaries, one for each set of mysteries. The married couple who spent a full hour gazing at Jesus together. The priest who did nothing but ask Jesus for guidance and wisdom as he tried to lead his parish.

If you answered "all of the above," then you're right. Any time that we go out of our way to visit Jesus, we will be blessed. Of course, not all of these kinds of visits are the same, and they don't all yield the same results. After all, we're talking about a relationship here, and in any relationship, there are degrees of intimacy.

If we simply sit before the Lord for an hour, then we will be blessed. We will feel good about what we have done, and we will leave our time with him feeling strengthened. Yet this approach to adoration has its limits. By preparing ourselves to meet the Lord and by having some knowledge of how the Holy Spirit works, we can increase our chances of receiving more from the Lord and of being changed more into his likeness. So let's look at a few ways we can approach adoration to see how the Spirit works in each of them.

Fix Your Eyes on Jesus. *Look to Jesus the pioneer and perfecter of our faith, who for the sake of the joy that was set before him endured the cross, disregarding its shame, and has taken his seat at the right hand of the throne of God. (Hebrews 12:2)*

The idea of fixing our eyes on Jesus is so simple that even a young child can understand it. As you kneel or sit before the Lord, call to mind your favorite images of Jesus. Some like to see him with his Blessed Mother, perhaps in their home at Nazareth or at the wedding feast of Cana. Others enjoy seeing Jesus at the Transfiguration, radiant with God's glory as he talks with Moses and Elijah. Still others prefer to see him feeding the five thousand or healing the hemorrhaging woman. Many people hold two images of Jesus dear to their hearts: the crucified Christ and the risen Lord seated at the right hand of his Father in glory.

When we begin to fix our eyes on one of these images and focus our attention on Jesus in the Sacrament, a couple of things begin to happen. First, the distractions of normal life, with all of its responsibilities, problems, and demands, fade away. Second, we begin to feel as if we have entered into heaven. We feel as if we too are "seated" with Jesus "in the heavenly places" (Ephesians 2:6). We get a taste of what it will be like when there will be no more suffering or pain, when we will be reunited with all of our loved ones, and when every hope and dream of ours will finally be fulfilled.

Listening for His Voice. *I pray that the God of our Lord Jesus Christ, the Father of glory, may give you a spirit of wisdom and revelation as you come to know him. (Ephesians 1:17)*

As we fix our eyes on Jesus in this way, something marvelous begins to happen. The Holy Spirit begins to open our minds and fill us with spiritual wisdom and understanding (Colossians 1:9). We begin to grasp more about Jesus: what he did for us, how much he loves us, how merciful he is, and how much he rejoices with us and suffers with us.

Words from Scripture that previously had little or no meaning begin to come alive. They enlighten our minds and urge us to be holy. They convince us that we have God's strength to help us and to make us more fruitful for Jesus.

Then comes the best part. Whatever we learn and understand moves us to love Jesus more. When we grasp who he is and what he has done for us, our only response is to say, "Jesus, I love you." We fall in love with him all over again, and his love in turn calms our fears, heals our wounds, and energizes us with hope and confidence. Some who find this intimacy have even felt Jesus putting his arms around them and holding them close to his heart.

Overcoming the World. *Little children, you are from God, and have conquered them; for the one who is in you is greater than the one who is in the world. (1 John 4:4)*

Another work of the Holy Spirit that frequently occurs as we adore Jesus in the Blessed Sacrament is directed toward the obstacles that block our way to God. St. Paul calls these obstacles "strongholds" that are raised up "against the knowledge of God" (2 Corinthians 10:4-5).

As we kneel before the Lord, we begin to hear the Holy Spirit gently tell us that perfection cannot be united with imperfection. He tells us that in Christ we have been made holy, and that we should now live as the holy man or woman he has made us to be. Suddenly, we find God's mercy and power working in us, helping us to take these strongholds captive and demolish them one by one, over time. We find God's grace working in us, convincing us that we can overcome everything that separates us from him.

As we are moved to repentance and confession, something inside of us—yes, it is the Holy Spirit—infuses us with a divine conviction and power. We leave our time of adoration convinced that we can stop sinning, and we find a new and greater ability to say "no" to the temptations that assail us in the course of our day.

Building the Kingdom of God. *I pray that you may lead lives worthy of the Lord, fully pleasing to him, as you bear fruit in every good work and as you grow in the knowledge of God. (Colossians 1:10)*

Like every parent, our heavenly Father has the perfect happiness of every human being in the forefront of his mind. Today, as happy as he is that we have come and spent time in Jesus' presence, he also gives us a taste of his sadness. If we look at Jesus long enough and closely enough, we can see him weeping over all the pain and suffering in the world. We can see him mourning over all the sin. We can see him weeping over those who reject him or who have never heard of him.

The pain that we see in the broken heart of Jesus moves us to take up his call. Adoration before Jesus moves us to say: "Here am I; send me" (Isaiah 6:8). It convinces us that our life with Jesus is about personal holiness and about being his light to everyone we meet.

The Holy Spirit wants to use our time of adoration to open our eyes to the needs of the poor, to the despair of the uneducated, to the loneliness of the unevangelized, and to the suffering and fears of the ill, the forgotten, and the homeless. The Spirit wants us to love Jesus so much that we feel compelled to serve him.

With Opened Eyes. To those who have never sat before the Lord in this way, Eucharistic adoration can seem like a waste of time. And yet to those who have tasted the goodness of the Lord, adoration has the power to move us closer to Jesus.

Think about Jesus' encounter with the Samaritan woman described in John 4. At the very beginning of their conversation, Jesus told her, "If you knew the gift of God, and who it is that is saying to you, 'Give me a drink,' you would have asked him, and he would have given you living water" (John 4:10). In a similar manner, Eucharistic adoration is not about our giving Jesus a drink by giving up our time to be with him as much as it is about our coming to Jesus and asking him for a drink. It's about presenting our needs to the Lord and asking him to fill us up with heavenly grace and heavenly power and heavenly wisdom. It's about receiving all that we need to live in him and for him in this world.

The more we fix our eyes on Jesus, the more we will appreciate how much he goes out of his way to reach us. When we come and meet him in adoration, he shows us—just as he showed the Samaritan woman—that he wants to be our Lord, our Savior, and our friend. As our eyes are opened, we will take his advice and ask him for a drink of his living water. And we will never be the same again. ■

LOVE IS BLIND

....

HOW DOES JESUS SEE US?

A recent study by scientists at University College in London gave proof to the saying that love is blind. Researchers studying the brain found that feelings of love can lead to a suppression of activity in the areas of the brain that control critical and judgmental thoughts.

The researchers monitored the brain activity of twenty young mothers as they were shown pictures of their children and of their loved ones. In both cases, the pictures produced increased positive feelings in the women, along with significantly reduced levels of activity in the part of the brain that controls negative judgments.

Commenting on their findings, lead scientist Dr. Andreas Bartels said, "Our research enables us to conclude that human attachment . . . deactivates networks used for critical social assessment and negative emotions, while it bonds individuals through the involvement of the 'reward circuitry,' explaining the power of love to motivate and exhilarate."

His Love Is Blind. So what does all this scientific jargon have to do with Eucharistic adoration? Simply this: When we come before Jesus in the Blessed Sacrament, we are not the only ones doing the looking and gazing. Jesus himself fixes his gaze on us, and as he looks at us, he is filled with such love and passion that it is as if his love is just as "blind" as the love of the young mothers in the study. When he sees us, Jesus is filled with an over-abundance of tenderness, mercy, love, and affection.

Of course, Jesus is not really blind. Naturally, he sees the anger, the jealousy, the lust, or the greed that is lurking in our hearts. But he also looks beyond these faults and failings. His vision penetrates deeper, and it ranges wider than our sin. He also sees our deepest longings for love, our hidden desires for holiness, and even his own plans and intentions to transform us and fill us with his divine life and power.

Think of some famous sinners in the Bible who allowed God's loving gaze to pierce their hearts.

Over and over again, Jesus' look of love simply melted away the sin and filled people with the hope of a new beginning.

There was the "sinful woman" in Luke 7:36-50, who anointed Jesus' feet and wiped them with her hair. There was the prodigal son, who was reinstated to sonship with no strings attached (15:11-32). There was Matthew, the tax collector, who left his livelihood to follow Jesus (Matthew 9:9-13). Even Peter, at one point filled with guilt over having denied knowing Jesus, was reinstated—no questions asked—when Jesus fixed his loving gaze on him (21:15-17). Over and over again, Jesus' look of love simply melted away the sin and filled people with the hope of a new beginning.

When you come to Jesus in Eucharistic adoration, remember one thing: His loving gaze is already fixed on you. Yes, you may need to repent for your sins. Yes, you may need to fix some broken or divided relationships. Yes, you may need inner healing over past hurts. But whether you are perfectly right with Jesus or not—and being right is, of course, a better position—he sees and dwells on all that is good and beautiful and commendable in you.

We Bring Jesus Joy. So this is what Jesus sees. But what does he think or feel when he sees us this way? Joy. Happiness. Love.

It has always been this way. Centuries before Christ, when God was confronting the people of Israel with numerous infidelities, he spoke a surprising word through the prophet Hosea. Rather than pledges of judgment, punishment, and wrath, God asked:

> How can I give you up, Ephraim? How can I hand you over, O Israel? My heart recoils within me; my compassion grows warm and tender. I will not execute my fierce anger; I will not again destroy Ephraim. For I am God and no mortal, the Holy One in your midst, and I will not come in wrath. (Hosea 11:8-9)

If a sinful nation can still move God to tenderness and compassion, and if little children can fill Jesus' heart with love and joy, imagine how much happiness we bring to Jesus! We are trying to do what is right. We want to be pleasing to the Lord—even if we are not always successful. Simply to come to him during a time of adoration must bring a smile to his face!

Again, when little children wanted to be with Jesus, he happily welcomed them and blessed them. He even told his disciples that the kingdom of heaven belongs to those who come to him like little children (Mark 10:13-15).

Finally, let's take a look at another woman who poured perfume over Jesus. In this story, Jesus was eating dinner at a friend's house when a woman came in with an alabaster jar of very expensive perfume. She broke the jar and poured the perfume on Jesus' head, letting the ointment run down his hair. Some who saw this extravagant act became indignant and rebuked her. "Why was the ointment wasted in this way?" they asked. "It could have been sold for more than three hundred denarii, and the money given to the poor." But Jesus told them to leave her alone. "She has performed a good service for me" (Mark 14:3-7).

Our lives are like that expensive perfume. It pleases the Lord when we pour out our lives in service to the poor, the sick, and the hurting. But at the same time, Jesus also loves it when we pour out our lives on him in love and worship. He is so happy when we come to him in adoration and "waste" our time, our attention, and our lives gazing upon him and letting him gaze upon us.

> **W**hen we open ourselves to his loving gaze, he gives us a taste of who we can become in him.

Taking the Long View. So far, we've spoken about how Jesus sees beyond our sin to who he created and intends us to be. We've also spoken about how much joy we bring to his heart when we spend time adoring him in the Blessed Sacrament. Now let's look at one final point. When we visit Jesus, he rejoices over all that we are doing for him. He never says, "It's not enough. You need to serve me more." He never says, "You're not faithful enough to me. You need to work harder." Rather, he blesses us and pours out his love on us, knowing that this is enough to compel us. He tells us how pleased he is with us, and that experience of God's pleasure motivates us to lay down even more of our lives. To put it more simply, his love for us calls more love out of us.

Jesus sees how we will be over time. He sees our potential. He knows all of our talents. And when we open ourselves to his loving gaze, he gives us a taste of who we can become in him. He gives us a glimpse of what life will be like when we are finally united with him forever. And in that glimpse, he tells us, "I can't wait for the day when you will be with me in heaven. I can't wait for the day when you will share fully in my love and goodness." It may be hard to believe, but Jesus is even more eager to be with us than we are to be with him!

Enjoy the Love of Jesus. If you stand next to someone who has put on too much perfume, you'll find that some of the scent actually clings to you after that person has gone. That's one way of thinking about what happens when we are with Jesus in Eucharistic adoration. The aroma of his holiness rubs off on us. It lifts us up to heaven, even as it makes us more pleasing and attractive to the people around us.

During Eucharistic adoration, trust that Jesus loves you and that he is pleased with your coming to be with him.

So during Eucharistic adoration, trust that Jesus loves you and that he is pleased with your coming to be with him. Trust that he dwells on who you are in him, and not as you typically think of yourself. See how he overlooks your failings and simply enjoys being near to you. Know that he has a super-abundance of love and peace to pour upon you. And finally, dare to believe that you bring joy to his heart simply by coming to sit at his feet and gaze upon him in love. ■

QUESTIONS FOR PERSONAL REFLECTION
AND FAITH SHARING:

■ Do you find it difficult to believe in Jesus' proclamation in John 6:51: "I am the living bread that came down from heaven. Whoever eats of this bread will live forever; and the bread that I will give for the life of the world is my flesh"? If so, why? What could help you to accept Jesus' words in faith?

■ Think of an occasion when you felt that Christ particularly touched you, spoke to you, or transformed you as you spent time before him in Eucharistic adoration. In what areas of your life do you see the fruits of time spent in Jesus' presence?

GUIDANCE FOR PRAYER AND ACTION:

■ As soon as you can, spend some time in adoration before the Blessed Sacrament. As you kneel or sit in the Jesus' Eucharistic presence in the tabernacle or in the monstrance, recall the words of Pope Benedict XVI:

> [Eucharistic] adoration means saying: "Jesus, I am yours. I will follow you in my life, I never want to lose this friendship, this communion with you." I could also say that adoration is essentially an embrace with Jesus in which I say to him: "I am yours, and I ask you, please stay with me always." (Catechetical meeting with children who had received their First Communion during the year, October 15, 2005)

■ Ask the Holy Spirit to guide you in expressing— either spontaneously or in writing—a prayer of gratitude and thanksgiving to Jesus for the precious gift of himself given to you in the Eucharist.

This booklet was published by The Word Among Us. Since 1981, The Word Among Us has been answering the call of the Second Vatican Council to help Catholic laypeople encounter Christ in the Scriptures.

The name of our company comes from the prologue to the Gospel of John and reflects the vision and purpose of all of our publications: to be an instrument of the Spirit, whose desire is to manifest Jesus' presence in and to the children of God. In this way, we hope to contribute to the Church's ongoing mission of proclaiming the gospel to the world so that all people would know the love and mercy of our Lord and grow ever more deeply in love with him.

Our monthly devotional magazine, *The Word Among Us*, features meditations on the daily and Sunday Mass readings, and currently reaches more than one million Catholics in North America and another half million Catholics in one hundred countries around the world. Our book division, The Word Among Us Press, publishes numerous books, Bible studies, and pamphlets that help Catholics grow in their faith.

To learn more about who we are and what we publish, log on to our website at www.wau.org. There you will find a variety of Catholic resources that will help you grow in your faith.

Embrace His Word, Listen to God . . .

www.wau.org